THE BRAIN BEHIND WEALTH

ILLUSTRATION ON ABUNDANCE, SELFISHNESS AND JOY

JONATHON SANCHEZ

TABLE OF CONTENT

Chapter 1
Understanding Finance

What Is Money?

Finance is a term for issues concerning the administration, creation, and investigation of cash and speculations. It includes the utilization of credit and obligation, protections, and venture to back current tasks utilizing future pay streams. Due to this transient perspective, finance is firmly connected to the time worth of cash, loan fees, and other related points.

Finance is a term extensively portraying the review and arrangement of cash, speculations, and other monetary instruments. While it has been established in logical fields, like measurements, financial aspects, and science, finance additionally incorporates non-logical components that

compare it to craftsmanship.

Finance incorporates banking, influence or obligation, credit, capital business sectors, cash, speculations, and the creation and oversight of monetary frameworks. Finance is characterized as the administration of cash and incorporates exercises like financial planning, getting, loaning, planning, saving, and anticipating. finance, the method involved with raising assets or capital for any sort of consumption. Customers, business firms, and state-run administrations frequently don't have the assets accessible to make consumptions, pay their obligations, or complete different exchanges and should get or offer value. Savers and financial backers, then again, gather supports that could acquire interest or profits whenever put to useful use.

These investment funds might gather as investment funds stores, reserve funds, credit offers, or benefits and protection claims; when lent out at revenue or put resources into value shares, they give a wellspring of venture reserves. Finance is the most common way of diverting these assets as credit, advances, or contributed money to those financial substances that most need them or can put them to the most useful use. The foundations that channel assets from savers to clients are called monetary mediators. They incorporate business banks, investment funds banks, reserve funds, and advance affiliations, and such nonbank establishments as credit associations, insurance agencies, benefits reserves, venture organizations, and money organizations.

Money can be comprehensively isolated into three classes:
- Public money
- Corporate money
- Individual budget

There are numerous other explicit classes. For example, conduct finance, which looks to recognize the mental (e.g., close to home, social, and mental) purposes for monetary choices. Essentially, our focus here is on individual accounting, as I will show you specialized tips and outlines to control your money.

Public Money

The national government forestalls market disappointment by administering the assignment of assets, dispersion of pay, and adjustment of the economy. Normal financing for these projects is gotten for the most part through tax collection. Acquiring from banks, insurance agencies, and different state-run administrations and procuring profits from its organizations likewise assist with supporting the national government. State and neighborhood legislatures likewise get awards and help from the central government. Different wellsprings of public money incorporate client charges from ports, air terminal administrations, and different offices; fines coming about because of overstepping regulations; incomes from licenses and expenses.

Corporate Money

Organizations get supporting through various means, going from value speculations to credit plans. A firm could apply for a line of credit from a bank or sort out a credit extension. Getting and overseeing obligations appropriately can help an organization grow and turn out to be more productive. New businesses might get capital from private supporters or financial speculators in return for a level of possession. On the off chance that an organization flourishes and opens up to the world, it will give shares on a stock trade; such starting public contributions (Initial public offering) bring an extraordinary convergence of money into a firm. Organizations might buy profit-paying stocks, blue-chip bonds, or premium-bearing bank authentications of stores (Cd); they

may likewise purchase different organizations with an end goal to support income.

Individual accounting

Individual monetary involves scrutinizing a person's or a family's Present monetary position, anticipating present moment, and long stretch requirements, and executing a course of action to fulfill those necessities inside individual financial prerequisites. Individual accounting relies generally upon one's profit, living necessities, and individual objectives and wants. Matters of individual accounting incorporate yet are not restricted to, the buying of monetary items for individual reasons, similar to Mastercards; life and home protection; home loans; and retirement items. Individual banking (e.g., checking and investment

accounts, IRAs, and 401(k) plans) is likewise viewed as a piece of an individual budget.

Individual budget, as a term, covers the ideas of dealing with your cash, saving, and effective money management. It additionally incorporates banking, planning, contracts, speculations, protection, retirement arranging, and expense arranging. One can consider that an individual budget includes the whole business that offers monetary types of assistance to people and prompts them about monetary and venture opportunities. Personal finance, as a term, covers the ideas of dealing with your cash, saving, and money management. It additionally incorporates banking, planning, contracts, speculations, protection, retirement arranging, and assessment

arranging. One can consider that individual budget includes the whole business that offers monetary types of assistance to people and exhorts them about monetary and speculation amazing open doors.

An individual budget is generally about acknowledging individual monetary objectives, whether it's saving enough for momentary monetary necessities, making retirement arrangements, or putting something aside for your kid's advanced degree. For the most part, it relies upon your pay, costs, living necessities, and individual objectives, and the arrangement you make to satisfy those objectives inside your monetary imperatives. Individual accounting manages family spending plans, the speculation of individual investment funds, and the utilization of purchaser credit. People normally acquire contracts from business banks and reserve funds and advance the relationship to buy their homes, while supporting the acquisition of customer strong products (cars, apparatuses) can be gotten from banks and monetary organizations. Charge records and Visas are other significant means by which banks and organizations stretch out momentary credit to shoppers. On the off chance that people need to solidify their obligations or acquire cash in a crisis, little money advances can be gotten at banks, credit associations, or money organizations.

It's vital to turn out to be monetarily proficient to take full advantage of your pay and reserve funds. Monetary education assists you with recognizing great and awful monetary exhortation and settling on wise choices. Hardly any schools offer seminars on dealing with your cash, so it is critical to gain proficiency with the essentials through free web-based articles, courses, web journals, digital broadcasts, or at the library. The new idea, shrewd individual accounting includes creating systems that incorporate planning, making a backup stash, taking care of obligations, utilizing Visas admirably, and putting something aside for retirement, from there, the sky is the limit.

The main parts of individual accounting include:

- Surveying the ongoing monetary status: expected income, current investment funds, and so on.
-

- Purchasing protection to safeguard against risk and to guarantee one's material standing is secure.
- Ascertaining and documenting charges
- Reserve funds and speculations
- Retirement arranging

As a specific field, individual budget is a new turn of events, however, types of it have been shown in colleges and schools as "home financial matters" or "shopper financial aspects" since the mid-twentieth 100 years. The field was at first dismissed by male business analysts, as "home financial matters" seemed, by all accounts, to be the domain of housewives. As of late, business analysts have more than once pushed far and wide training in issues of individual accounting as necessary to the large-scale execution of the general public economy.

Social Money

Social money regularly alludes to ventures made in friendly endeavors including beneficent associations and a few cooperatives. As opposed to a by and large gift, these ventures appear as value or obligation funding, in which the financial backer looks for both monetary compensation as well as a social increase. Present-day types of social money likewise incorporate a few sections of microfinance, explicitly credits to entrepreneurs and business people in less evolved nations to empower their ventures to develop. Banks procure a profit from their credits while at the same time assisting with working on people's way of life and helping the neighborhood society and economy. Social influence bonds (otherwise called Pay for Progress Bonds or social advantage bonds) are a particular sort of instrument that goes about as an agreement with the public area or nearby government. Reimbursement and profit from speculation are dependent upon the accomplishment of specific social results and accomplishments.

Conduct Money

Sometime in the past hypothetical and experimental proof implied that regular monetary speculations were sensibly effective at foreseeing and making sense of specific sorts of financial occasions. In any case, as time went on, scholastics in the monetary and financial domains recognized irregularities and ways of behaving which happened in reality yet couldn't be made sense of by any suitable hypotheses. It turned out to be progressively evident that customary speculations could make sense of certain "romanticized" occasions — yet that this present reality was, as a matter of fact, significantly more muddled and complicated, and that market members habitually act in unreasonable manners, and hence hard to foresee as per those models.

Thus, scholastics started to go to mental brain research to represent nonsensical and irrational ways of behaving which are unexplained by the current monetary hypothesis. Conduct science is the field that was conceived out of these endeavors; it looks to make sense of our activities, though present-day finance tries to make sense of the activities of the glorified "monetary man" (Homo economics). Social money, a sub-field of conducting financial matters, proposes brain research-based speculations to make sense of monetary irregularities, like serious ascents or falls in stock cost. The design is to distinguish and comprehend the reason why individuals pursue specific monetary decisions. Inside social money, it is accepted the data structure and the attributes of market members efficiently impact people's venture choices as well as market results.

CHAPTER 2
Concepts of selfishness

Childishness intertwined with selfishness is being concerned exorbitantly or solely, for oneself or one's a benefit, delight, or government assistance, paying little heed to other people. Childishness is something contrary to unselfishness or benevolence.

The research proposes that self-centeredness depends on a person's close to home and mental requirements. Much of the time, the childish individual has a large number of similar qualities to somebody who is narcissistic. The disposition is that of a "taker" and not a harmony producer. The disposition may likewise be inactive forceful, tricky, and unreasonable. Most people who show childish character attributes scarcely at any point consider what they mean for or influence others around them. The ones who do frequently figure out how to cover their self-centeredness with shallow appeal and consideration.

The world spins around them and them as it were. Certain individuals show ways of behaving that you could never envision. The way of behaving of somebody who is narrow-minded depends on falsehoods and the absence of capacity to consider the prosperity of others. It tends to be negative, most definitely.

The demeanor is that of a "taker" and not

a harmony producer. The demeanor may likewise be aloof forceful, tricky, and unreasonable.

Childish individuals struggle with thinking often about anybody yet themselves. They're not simply being inconsiderate when they couldn't care less, it's really beyond the realm of possibilities for them to focus on another person's requirements over their own. Self-centered individuals can be rough and awkward to communicate with along these lines.

Self-fixation implies we are more inclined to stress and psychological wellness issues. Narrow-mindedness might make it simpler for us to fall into traps like enslavement. Our self-centeredness can mean we hurt others as we heartlessly endeavor to fulfill our necessities. Conceit can harm our standing and lead to forlornness.

Childishness truly appears to have its foundations in the term self-absorption. A way of behaving is both hereditary and ecological. It is kept up with by intrinsic propensities and affected by demeanor as well as outer gaining from guardians and others all through youngster improvement. I'm of the firm conviction that narrow-mindedness can likewise be impacted by unfortunate family/social qualities or insignificantly communicated values by grown-ups all through a youngster's turn of events. As such, kids who are brought up in a climate of childish addition and absence of values are bound to become egotistical. For instance, kids who are brought up in a climate of the steady quest for material abundance (without the quest major areas of strength for) are probably going to form into childish, self-centered grown-ups.

Childishness is many times viewed as a bothersome or even corrupt trademark, while benevolence is commonly thought to be all-around attractive and temperate. Nonetheless, mankind's set of experiences as well as crafted by humanistic and psychodynamic therapists highlight a more intricate picture: not all childishness is essentially terrible, and not all benevolence is fundamentally great. Childishness is generally connected with an intentional demonstration. For instance, a self-centered individual purposely centers around their plan, instead of that of others. The demonstration of being childish can likewise be oblivious or coincidental. This kind of childishness is no less legitimate and may be more horrendous to general society, because of its more subtle nature. Instances of oblivious narrow-mindedness might be so little as to not be seen, yet frequently happen in huge amounts.

Narrow-mindedness is the inclination to focus on one's longings and necessities over the requirements and wants of others. We are undeniably brought into the world with a drive to remain alive and sound, and self-centeredness might be a lost indication of this. A specific level of self-centeredness is typical. For instance, many individuals would decide to guarantee their own food needs are met before giving food to other people. However, childishness can likewise be an obsessive character quality. Self-centered individuals might focus on their trivial necessities over the huge requirements of others. For instance, an individual is displaying childishness when the person takes cash from their mom to purchase a comic book.

Some psychological well-being issues can add to the advancement of narrow-mindedness. Numerous behavioral conditions, especially total disregard for other people and self-absorbed behavioral conditions, make individuals so enveloped with their cravings that they either don't see or couldn't care less about the requirements of others. Numerous other psychological instabilities can cause outrageous self-inclusion, which can add to childishness. A discouraged individual, for instance, may be so enveloped with the sensations of experiencing that he/she can't accommodate his/his kids or speak with his/her accomplice. It is usually accepted that ethical quality requests we pick between forfeiting others to ourselves (which is considered "childish" and along these lines unethical) and forfeiting our qualities to fulfill others' necessities (which is considered unselfish and subsequently upright).

Narrow-mindedness, nonetheless, doesn't imply "doing anything you please." Moral standards are not an issue of closely-held conviction — they are situated in current realities of the real world, in man's temperament as a normal being, who should think and act effectively to live and be blissful. Profound quality's errand is to recognize the sorts of activity that benefit oneself. These ideals (efficiency, autonomy, respectability, trustworthiness, equity, pride) are utilizations of the essential uprightness, and discernment.

Chapter 3
The brain behind wealth

The production of riches and accomplishing monetary well-being includes more than information-driven bookkeeping sheets. There are social dangers along the way of abundance creation that can influence both the individuals who have currently effectively amassed abundance as well as those seeking to expand their total assets. Abundance is in many cases made or obliterated in light of our ways of behaving and the human way of behaving is everything except basic. Our monetary ways of behaving are established in our previous encounters, our attitude, and our convictions about cash, which can prompt silly cash choices in light of profound affiliations connected with cash. We frequently have factors neutralizing us with regards to using wise judgment connected with acquiring, saving, spending, effective money management, and continuing through to the end toward monetary autonomy as well as keeping up with and passing on abundance whenever it is accomplished.

An abundance mentality implies spending less, making wise speculations, and searching for ways of working on money remaining with a negligible gamble. Fortunately, with just the right amount of devotion, anybody can foster this outlook. If you dig further into the tales of rich individuals, you'll see a theme: Seldom can a rich individual reduce their prosperity to a solitary marvelous second? All things being equal, they'll refer to their attitude as the main motivation for their flourishing. An abundance outlook is a bunch of convictions, propensities, and ways of behaving that isolate the well-off from the rest. An abundance outlook will direct you to capitalize on the cash you have. Be that as it may, it doesn't come simple. An abundance mentality implies spending less, making wise ventures, and searching for ways of working on money remaining with an insignificant gamble.

The Brain Research of Cash investigates how cash moves around in an economy and how private predispositions and the profound variable assume a significant part in our monetary choices, as well as how to naturally suspect all the more soundly and settle on better choices with regards to cash. Our individual accounting records assume a colossal part in our lives. But individuals seldom talk about them and instruct themselves on this point. Thus, numerous assumptions and misleading thoughts regarding cash have arisen throughout the long term. They think having cash is a consequence of karma or that rich individuals are inheritors. Or on the other hand, maybe abundance has a place just with the individuals who upset the world and advantage from their revelations.

Wrong! Cash is a general, round resource on the planet. Furthermore, you also can turn out to be monetarily free, in the event that you decide to take on a couple of abundance developing practices and significantly impact your ongoing mentality. From the beginning, you'll need to recognize what is going on. Disrupt the general flow between your ongoing life and the existence you want one-sided monetary choices.
Then, at that point, it'll be more straightforward to detect and dispose of them. Your approaches to looking for status, your jealousy, and different feelings that have command over all of you

assume a huge part regards your monetary choices. Obviously, there are different things to investigate with regards to making better decisions with your cash.

Being ravenous can end up being the greatest monetary mix-up you'll at any point make. Envy is not welcome in the currency market, as it can obscure your reasoning. Our initial encounters with cash decide our monetary choices later on. With regards to cash and putting resources into general, there are sure factors that we ought to consider and figure out how to control to become effective. Other than envy, anxiety toward passing up a great opportunity is one of them. At the point when you assess your ventures and decide to put specific exchanges, you need to stay with them through great and awful.

In the event that you're moderately youthful and procure more than you spend, the most ideal way to upgrade your drawn-out speculation returns is to put most of your cash into a differentiated arrangement of minimal expense list reserves. Holding in excess of a couple of rate points of your total assets in real money is senseless on the grounds that the worth of money dissolves with expansion, and that money can in any case be placed into resources like stocks that generally have accumulated at a pace of 6-7%.

While a charming possibility to put resources into ways that amplify your profits, these speculations frequently don't represent your brain science. Envision you're 95% put resources into stocks and have 5% in real money. The market declines by 20-25%. Contingent upon what that crash means for your brain research, having such a little rate in real money might make you bound to overreact and sell a portion of your stocks during that slump. Furthermore, that frenzy sell might prompt you to pass up definitely a greater number of profits than if you had held a bigger level of your portfolio in real money and didn't sell since you had a solid sense of reassurance.

Subsequently, the profound element is quite possibly the main thing you can chip away at if you have any desire to turn out to be monetarily free. Continuously recall that your process will be not the same as some other individual you know or know about, so there's compelling reason need to contrast yourself with them or be envious of anybody's more prominent resources. Creating financial momentum after some time involves following three essential advances and adhering to them. The initial step is to bring in sufficient cash to cover your necessities, with some leftover for saving. The subsequent step is to deal with your spending so you can amplify your investment funds. The third step is to put your cash in a wide range of resources so that it's appropriately differentiated for the long stretch.

Figuring out 3 Straightforward Moves toward Creating Financial stability

Stage 1: Bring in Cash

This step might appear to be rudimentary however the most major one for

individuals who are simply beginning is. You've presumably seen outlines showing that a limited quantity of cash consistently saved and permitted to intensify over the long haul ultimately can develop into a significant total. Yet, those diagrams never answer this fundamental inquiry: How would you get cash to save in any case?

There are two essential approaches to bringing in cash: procured pay or automated revenue.

Procured pay comes from how you make ends meet, while recurring, automated revenue is gotten from ventures. You might not have any recurring, automated revenue until you've brought in sufficient cash to start money management.

If you are either going to begin a vocation or mulling over a profession change, these inquiries might assist you with settling on what you believe should do — and where your procured pay will come from: What do you appreciate? You will perform better, form a more drawn-out enduring profession, and be bound to succeed monetarily by accomplishing something that you appreciate and see as significant. One investigation discovered that more than nine out of 10 specialists said they would exchange a level of their lifetime profit for more noteworthy importance at work. What are you great at? Take a gander at what you get along admirably and how you can utilize those gifts to make money. What will compensate fairly? See vocations utilizing what you appreciate and do well that will measure up to your monetary assumptions. One great wellspring of compensation data, as well as the development possibilities for different fields, is the yearly Word-related Standpoint Handbook distributed by the U.S.

Stage 2: Set aside Cash

Bringing in cash won't assist you with creating financial well-being assuming that you wind up spending everything. To save more cash for creating financial stability, think about these four maneuvers:

- **Track your spending for essentially a month.** You should utilize a monetary programming bundle to assist you with doing this, however, a little, pocket-size scratch pad could likewise do the trick. Record all your uses, regardless of how little; many individuals are shocked to see where all their cash goes.

- **Track down the fat and trim it.** Separate your consumptions into requirements and needs. Food, sanctuary, and attire are clear requirements. Add medical coverage expenses to that rundown, alongside collision protection assuming you own a vehicle and live coverage on the off chance that others are reliant upon your pay. Numerous different

consumptions will just be needed. Be that as it may, seriously investigate the two classifications. While you can presumably take out certain needs through and through, you might be spending more than you truly should on certain requirements, like apparel.

- **Put forth an investment funds objective.** This doesn't imply that you need to live like a penny pincher or be economical constantly. If you're meeting your reserve funds objectives, go ahead and reward yourself and go overboard (a fitting sum) every so often. You'll feel improved and be roused to remain on track.

- **Put saving money on programmed.** One simple method for saving a limited sum every month is to orchestrate with your manager or bank to consequently move a specific part of every check into different reserve funds or speculation accounts. Also, you can put something aside for retirement by having cash consequently removed from your compensation and put into your boss' 401(k) or comparative arrangement. Monetary organizers ordinarily encourage sufficiently contributing to get your boss' full matching commitment.

Remember this, as well: You can, unfortunately, cut a limited amount a lot of costs. If your expenses are now down deep down, you ought to investigate ways of expanding your pay.

Stage 3: Put away Cash

Whenever you've figured out how to save some cash, the subsequent stage is money management with the goal that it will develop.

(Before you begin money management, be that as it may, make sure you have some cash put away to deal with any surprising monetary crises. A typical proposal is to develop to the point of covering something like three to a half years of costs in a fluid record, for example, a bank account or a currency market reserve.) Speculations change regarding hazard and expected return. When in doubt, the more secure they are, the lower their likely return, as well as the other way around.

In the event that you're not currently acquainted with the different kinds of ventures, it merits investing a little energy in looking into them. While there is a wide range of fascinating ventures, a great many people will need to begin with the essentials: stocks, securities, and shared reserves. Stocks are portions of proprietorship in an organization. Stocks are for the most part considered more dangerous than bonds, however, stocks can likewise shift generally in risk starting with one enterprise and then onto the next. Bonds are like IOUs from an organization or government. At the point when you purchase a security, the guarantor vows to take care of your cash, with a premium, after a specific period. As an exceptionally overall guideline, bonds are viewed as safer than stocks, yet with less possible potential gain. Simultaneously, a few bonds are less secure than others; bond-rating offices dole out letter grades to mirror that.

Common assets are pools of protection — frequently stocks, bonds, or a mix of the two. Shared reserves additionally change in risk, contingent upon what they put resources into.

Maybe the main money management idea for novices (or any financial backer, besides) is broadening. Basically, your objective ought to be to spread your cash among various kinds of ventures. That is on the grounds that ventures perform distinctively at various times. For instance, on the off chance that the financial exchange is on a terrible streak, bonds might be giving great returns. Or on the other hand, if Stock an is struggling, Stock B might be on a tear.

Shared reserves give some underlying enhancement since they put resources into various protections. What's more, you'll accomplish more prominent expansion in the event that you put resources into both a stock asset and a security reserve (or a few stock assets and a few security assets), for instance, as opposed to in only either. An idea firmly connected with broadening is the resource portion. It includes concluding which level of your portfolio you need to put resources into every specific resource classification, or sort of safety, in light of chance and different elements. As another basic guideline, the more youthful you are, the more gamble you

can stand to take since you'll have more years to compensate for any misfortunes. Cash. Power. Popularity. Victory. All achievements in life that we've been told would be able "go to our head" — importance, in the colloquial sense, that we become vainglorious, hard, and oddly careless individuals who rooted for us and the spots from which we came.

Abundance mentality — or bountiful reasoning — is less about what we have and more about what we accept is accessible to us. Setting aside cash is hard — that is a logical reality.

Whether it's moving cash to a bank account or settling an obligation, taking savvy monetary actions can conflict with your most essential human senses, as per specialists who concentrate on how the mind responds to cash. So we asked two neuroscientists: how do our cerebrums help and thwart us in our monetary choices — and how might we utilize that information to carry on with a more extravagant life Figuring out how psychological well-being and cash are associated could help in the event that you're battling. Figuring things out could feel like a mind-boggling task. Also, loads of things might be beyond your control. Be that as it may, have a go at approaching things slowly and carefully.

CHAPTER 4
Wealth management

Abundance the board is a venture warning assistance that joins other monetary administrations to address the necessities of well-off clients. An abundance the board guide is an undeniable level proficient who deals with a well-off client's abundance comprehensively, ordinarily for one set expense. The issue is monetary abundance is an outer objective with benefits restricted to the world beyond you. Cash purchases things, however cash doesn't purchase satisfaction. It can construct you a prettier jail, yet it can't get you out of jail. The inborn furthest reaches of outside objectives (extravagant houses, vehicles, and enormous ledgers) likewise restrict how inspired you will be while chasing after them.

To prevail with regards to creating financial stability, you need to be driven by inside objectives more profound than simply the outside features of riches. You need a reason that will carry change to your life and drive you sufficiently profound to defeat every one of the hindrances that stand among you and independence from the rat race.

Inside-driven objectives that could

concentrate to the point of succeeding incorporate the accompanying:

- **Opportunity:** Loosen up from the shackles of everyday work with the goal that you have an additional opportunity to develop, make, and live to your fullest potential.

- **Good cause:** The more you have the more you can give. Magnanimous establishments made by well-off families frequently give the monetary muscle to engage incredible social and natural causes.

- **Development:** When you have independence from the rat race, you additionally have an additional opportunity to seek individual flexibility. The abundance in your outside world turns into a mirror to the abundance in your inner world. The rules that lead to monetary abundance can likewise prompt genuine abundance by influencing different aspects of your life.

- **Administration:** Develop your own abundance morally and blissfully so you can show others how it's done for loved ones to transcend the obligations of monetary unremarkableness and emulate your example. The explanation more profound causes are fundamental is on the grounds that creating financial stability is difficult.

You will experience numerous issues that should be defeated along your excursion to independence from the rat race. You will follow through on a cost to arrive at your objective.
The abundance of the executives is something other than speculation counsel. It can incorporate all pieces of an individual's monetary life. Rather than endeavoring to coordinate

Recommendations and different items from numerous experts, high total assets people might be bound to profit from an incorporated methodology. In this strategy, an abundance supervisor facilitates the administrations expected to deal with their client's resources, alongside making a smart course of action for their current and future requirements — whether it is will and trust administrations or business progression plans. Numerous abundance directors can offer types of assistance in any part of the monetary field, yet some decide to have practical experience specifically regions, like cross-line abundance the executives. This might be founded on the mastery of a particular abundance chief, or the essential focal point of the business inside which the abundance supervisor works.

On specific occasions, an abundance of the executive's guide might need to facilitate input from outside monetary specialists, as well as the client's own help experts (for instance, a lawyer or bookkeeper) to make the ideal methodology to help the client. Some abundance chiefs additionally give banking administrations or exhortation on humanitarian exercises. Abundance the board counsels in the immediate utility of a venture company might have more information in the space of speculation procedure, while who's employers a huge bank might zero in on the administration of trusts and accessible credit choices, generally home preparation, or protection choices. To put it plainly, aptitude might fluctuate across various firms.

The abundance of executives is the most elevated level of monetary arranging administrations. It by and large incorporates far-reaching venture the board close by monetary counsel, charge direction, home preparation, and, surprisingly, legitimate help. As a matter of fact, numerous confidential abundance directors will facilitate with other monetary specialists —, for example, bookkeepers or home arranging trained professionals — for the benefit of clients to offer far-reaching monetary counsel. The kind of administration presented by an abundance of the executives in the firm is the most ideal for wealthy clients. Yet, while you may not need an abundance of executives now, your requirements are probably going to change over the long haul. The abundance of executives is the most exceptional type of speculation counsel administration. An abundance counsel normally makes an extraordinarily fitted speculation technique and plan for their clients to assist them with dealing with their resources.

Abundance the board firms give monetary ability on complex monetary issues for rich clients regularly in the main one to three percent of U.S. family pay. Abundance supervisors deal with clients' venture portfolios and give definite monetary guidance on various issues and open doors. The abundance of the board is a sort of monetary warning help for licensed financial backers and others with high total assets. Abundance supervisors give guidance about money management, home preparation, expenses, and whatever else that can assist with growing a client's riches. By understanding how abundance the executives functions and how it thinks about resources the board can work on your monetary picture.

The issue of just paying attention to the incredibly fruitful is that they are outrageous anomalies and they typically have outrageous karma also. The counsel they give probably won't be for a wide crowd and it could have worked for them.

Achievement is a horrible guide, it shows you only one right way and permits you to fail to remember the mind-blowing takes a chance en route that might have been a millimeter away from collapsing all achievement. The line between chance and achievement is just a millimeter thick and in some cases must be seen looking back. Results are made of probabilities, seldom by certain things with 100 percent possibilities. In the event that you buy organization stock and it does ineffectively for a long time you might have pursued an unfortunate choice or you might have settled on a decent choice with an 80% possibility of working out, you coincidentally experienced the 20% component result.

Look for something incredible and plan for it. Never trust sure things. Continuously work in the best wiggle room and be adaptable in the plans you do have (By planning and not over-utilizing). You can lose a huge load of cash in light of the fact that an arrangement went 80% right when you wanted it to go 100 percent right. It's not being moderate essentially. Traditionalism is staying away from risk, leaving an edge for blunder is raising your odds of coming out on top given any circumstance of chance. Hopefulness isn't indiscriminately figuring all that will go right. It's trusting in yourself and your arrangement enough to realize that over the long haul, everything will pan out better. The best thing about the room for giving and taking is the more safety buffer you have, the more modest your benefits must be to outflank most.

The knowledge is the most ideal way to use your pay level isn't generally to increment it, once in a while the simplest and best system is to live inside your means and lessen spending.

You have not ensured expansions in pay consistently but rather assuming you lessen the spending you are ensured more reserve funds. The amount of your abundance is reliant upon the way of life you live. On the off chance that you spend less, and save more. Then you will get abundance at a much lower level than someone who spends a ton. Spending short of what you make and saving all the more likewise give you monetary adaptability. A significant benefit in the present society where open doors are not generally limited by region. Assuming have the opportunity and willpower to be patient and the adaptability to sit tight to extraordinary open doors, you can make the most of the ongoing economic

situations in work and ventures.
You don't need to put something aside for something explicit like a house or a vehicle. Simply save to save. Collect abundance for amassing opportunity.

Contributing is a delicate science, not hard science. In Science, you'd have the option to concentrate on a Kidney or DNA quite a while back and it would have similar qualities today yet showcases dislike this. Qualities from the past can see you a little about money management today however not the total picture. While arranging your venture technique, an absence of a creative mind can have horrendous outcomes.
The fact is history has its advantages to give a free aide of what to do in specific

conditions yet not considerably more. The farther you return, the less applicable points of interest become, rather center around the more extensive responses and outcomes of occasions, similar to human responses and general subjects. Try not to search for a bit-by-bit guide or points of interest.

Individuals will be in the contributing space going about as prophets utilizing many authentic data of interest yet consistently recollect that set of experiences might coordinate yet doesn't necessarily rehash the same thing. Particular troublesome occasions end up causing a greater part of world results and these occasions will be irregular and apparently out of the blue. Plan for the astonishment.

Everybody has an alternate methodology yet a great many people fail to remember that every individual is playing an alternate technique and they respond in light of another person's situation and procedure. Before you take guidance or pursue the direction of the market, ask yourself, "What is my procedure?" Disappointment can be a crummy instructor since it tempts brilliant individuals into thinking their choices were horrible when once in a while they simply mirror the unforgiving real factors of hazard."

Orchestrate your monetary life such that

a terrible venture here and a missed monetary objective there won't clear you out so you can continue to play until the chances fall in support of yourself. There is an iron regulation in financial matters: very great and incredibly awful conditions seldom remain as such for long on the grounds that organic markets adjust in difficult to-foresee ways. We let ourselves know stories to fill in the holes of what are really vulnerable sides. Conventional people with no monetary instruction can be well off on the off chance that they have a modest bunch of conduct abilities that don't have anything to do with formal proportions of knowledge. We as a whole suspect we know how the world functions, Yet we've all main encountered a small bit of it

CHAPTER 5
Managing Abundance, joy

Overflow isn't about overabundance. There's no need to focus on having far an overabundance. There's no need to focus on stuff. Stuff doesn't satisfy us. Stuff doesn't satisfy us or carry us nearer to our families or to God. Stuff just occupies the unfilled environments in our souls and psyches and leaves us without space for the things that really matter. Running against the norm, overflow is tied in with feeling profound fulfillment in our souls, brains, and spirits.

1. Remain Coordinated

One of the greatest ways I keep an outlook of overflow is by remaining coordinated. At the point when my life feels turbulent, I don't see the value in what I have. I wind up heading out to the

store to purchase something since I can't find the something I currently own. I feel overpowered and in a bad way. Very much like carriers advise you to put on your own breathing device before you help everyone around you — I must be coordinated and on top of my own family before I can begin to help any other person.

Assuming command over your timetable and home can assist you with assuming command over your life. It's more straightforward to serve and provide for others when you're ready to do as such. Maybe you've ceased inviting somebody into your home since you felt it was muddled, or maybe you felt terrible in light of the fact that you didn't have a

cooler feast to share or a gift close by when an extraordinary event emerged. Association is the way to develop a feeling of serenity and have positive expectations about having a technique for going after your objectives.
One astonishing result of being coordinated? You could find you have considerably more than you naturally suspected you did! Unexpectedly, you find gift vouchers you disregarded. You could find toys and games your children

didn't recall you own. You'll review a most loved outfit you haven't worn in months. At the point when you put together your home, it tends to resemble revealing lost treasure.

2. Center around the Positive

As I said previously, in the event that you can peruse this book, odds are you're in an ideal situation than a large part of the world. We approach to power, water, food, haven, and apparel. Here and there life is exceptionally difficult, agonizing, baffling, and hard. It tends to be extremely simple to fail to remember that on a major level, our fundamental necessities are normally being met.

3. Practice Appreciation

Every day, consider the things you're thankful for and set aside some margin to rehearse appreciation for God and to people around you. It's astonishing how

rehearsing appreciation can reexamine your viewpoint and alter your attitude about everything! At the point when my

children are agitated about something or feeling especially irritable, we frequently take a couple of seconds and think about a portion of the things we're blissful about and thankful for. Recognizing and "remembering your good fortune" can assist you with acknowledging the amount you possess. It likewise goes far in developing greater liberality.

Consider it: when you accomplish something pleasant for another person, you likely feel a warm gleam just from the demonstration… however when the

individual says thank you, you get another lift. Besides the fact that it gives

you a lift, yet odds are you're likely more able to help them over and over. Communicating thanks isn't just a great habit, it additionally keeps beneficial things streaming in your direction. Your attitude can profoundly influence the course of your life. Overpowering exploration on outlook shows that the manner in which you ponder yourself and your general surroundings can radically alter the manner in which you realize, how you handle pressure, how you make achievements, your flexibility, and even the way that you resist framework capabilities.

Since that time, cultivating an overflow

mentality has become generally perceived as a valuable undertaking in a private and profound turn of events. The

overall conviction is that making an overflow outlook permits you to:

Carry on with a limitless, full, and fulfilling life Radiate satisfaction notwithstanding the situation Give and get warm gestures and things of high worth effortlessly Feel copious, innovative, and roused.Make the most of and appreciate new open doors that come in your direction. Make noteworthy and significant educational encounters Have a real sense of reassurance and positive about your life tries and make effective results, Overflow implies bounty or an extremely enormous amount of something. It is the inborn propensity of nature and of life to show, develop, and become more. It is the

inclination of the existing power to deliver more and make a greater amount of everything. There are in every case new trees, new plants, more food, and new organizations.

New things are by and large continually imagined. New vehicles are being created. New houses are being constructed, and new positions are made. Researchers say that the Universe is continuously extending and developing, and, surprisingly, new stars are being made. This is bountifulness on an infinite level. Overflow implies plentitude, and it is wherever in the Universe. It can likewise show up in your own life, in the event that you let it. Overflow seems not just as a lot of cash, riches, and assets, as

a great many people think. It likewise appears in numerous alternate ways. It

can appear as a richness of affection, kinship, information, and wellbeing.
How do draw overflow into your life? To do so you really want to feel plentiful. You need to create "overflow awareness".

Envision that overflow is as of now appearing in some part of your life. Feel it, and partake in this inclination.
You could now inquire: "What to do in the event that I don't have any idea what I precisely need?" You could inquire, "I can't envision things plainly." The response is it doesn't make any difference. The inclination counts.
Simply feel bountiful and partake in the

inclination. Do so a few times each day, for a couple of moments. You don't have to envision what is going on or

object. Simply feel so great the plentitude is appearing in your life.
When you get an overflow attitude, your life is quieter and simpler to make due. The sensation of pushing harder and achieving more will start to die down, and you will just do the things expected of you to live effectively and cheerfully and according to your very own preferences. At the point when you have an overflow outlook, you will carry on with a significant existence unbounded, with no psychological limits, and boundless open doors. With an overflow outlook, you will be thankful for the

things you have and anticipate the chance of developing and bettering yourself time

permitting. This will diminish your nervousness and stress and give you a more inspirational perspective on life.

Genuine overflow is an encounter through which every one of our requirements can be met, and numerous of our cravings as a rule are unexpectedly satisfied. We know genuine overflow when we feel happiness, and delight, in each second of people's life. We are overseeing endless causes of supply. All that we want is sitting right checking us out. In the universe, there is no might be like shortage or need. There isn't any contest with any person. Your heart

needs are generally accessible given you
may be available to get them and offer

your gift to the world.

Genuine overflow is acknowledging bliss
from the nature of your encounters and
connections, paying little heed to how
much cash you acquire or the abundance
you amass. Cash is basically a device
that can straightforwardly or in a
roundabout way influence the nature of
those encounters and connections, no
matter what. Just seeking after cash for
aggregating a greater amount of it tends
to be counterproductive and may really
be unsafe to your wellbeing (e.g., stress)
and connections (e.g., dismissing key

individual connections by investing unnecessary energy in work that you don't see as significant or potentially isn't

in arrangement with your guiding principle).